1 MONTH OF
FREE
READING

at

www.ForgottenBooks.com

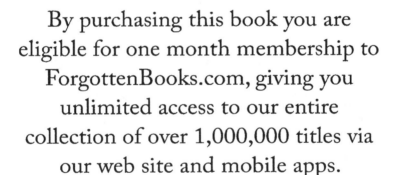

By purchasing this book you are eligible for one month membership to ForgottenBooks.com, giving you unlimited access to our entire collection of over 1,000,000 titles via our web site and mobile apps.

To claim your free month visit:

www.forgottenbooks.com/free922801

ISBN 978-0-260-02147-2
PIBN 10922801

This book is a reproduction of an important historical work. Forgotten Books uses state-of-the-art technology to digitally reconstruct the work, preserving the original format whilst repairing imperfections present in the aged copy. In rare cases, an imperfection in the original, such as a blemish or missing page, may be replicated in our edition. We do, however, repair the vast majority of imperfections successfully; any imperfections that remain are intentionally left to preserve the state of such historical works.

rofiche
ies
nographs)

Collection de microfiches (monographies)

Microreproductions / Institut canadien de microreproductions historiques

1995

The Institute has attempted to obtain the best original copy available for filming. Features of this copy which may be bibliographically unique, which may alter any of the images in the reproduction, or which may significantly change the usual method of filming, are checked below.

L'Institut a microfilmé le lui a été possible de se exemplaire qui sont bibliographiques, qui peuvent reproduite, ou qui peuvent dans la méthode normale de ci-dessous.

☐ Coloured covers/
Couverture de couleur

☐ Covers damaged/
Couverture endommagée

☐ Covers restored and/or laminated/
Couverture restaurée et/ou pelliculée

☐ Cover title missing/
Le titre de couverture manque

☐ Coloured maps/
Cartes géographiques en couleur

☐ Coloured ink (i.e. other than blue or black)/
Encre de couleur (i.e. autre que bleue ou noire)

☐ Coloured plates and/or illustrations/
Planches et/ou illustrations en couleur

☐ Bound with other material/
Relié avec d'autres documents.

☐ Tight binding may cause shadows or distortion along interior margin/
La reliure serrée peut causer de l'ombre ou de la distorsion le long de la marge intérieure

☐ Blank leaves added during restoration may appear within the text. Whenever possible, these have been omitted from filming/
Il se peut que certaines pages blanches, ajoutées lors d'une restauration apparaissent dans le texte, mais, lorsque cela était possible, ces pages n'ont pas été filmées.

☐ Coloured pages/
Pages de couleur

☐ Pages damaged/
Pages endommagées

☐ Pages restored and/or
Pages restaurées et/ou

☑ Pages discoloured,
Pages décolorées,

☐ Pages detached/
Pages détachées

☑ Showthrough/
Transparence

☑ Quality of print varies/
Qualité inégale de l'im

☐ Continuous pagination
Pagination continue

☐ Includes index(es)/
Comprend un (des)

Title on header taken
Le titre de l'en-tête

☐ Title page of issue/
Page de titre de la

☐ Caption of issue/
Titre de départ de la liv

☐ Masthead/
Générique (périodiques

2 3

2

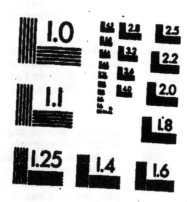

APPLIED IMAGE Inc

1653 East Main Street
Rochester, New York 14609 USA
(716) 482 - 0300 - Phone
(716) 288 - 5989 - Fax

The Liberal Point of View

Current Comment on the Proceedings of the Parliamentary Session of 1922.

NATIONAL LIBERAL COMMITTEE
115 Sparks Street,
OTTAWA.

HONORABLE W. L. MACKENZIE KING, M.P.,
Liberal Leader.

ANDREW HAYDON,
National Organiser and General Secretary.

JOHN LEWIS,
Editor of Liberal Publications.

Publication No. 4.   Issued June 15.

The New Taxes

The great need of the country at the present time is a revision of the tariff which will reduce the high cost of living. The Drayton budget increases the high cost of living. The Government makes a virtue of the fact that it is introducing direct taxation. There would be something in the claim if direct taxes were being substituted for indirect taxes. Here the direct taxes are piled on top of the indirect taxes ,and the consumer pays it all. A man goes into a store and buys a suit of clothes made of English cloth. The cloth has paid a high customs duty, made higher by the fact that the customs authorities insist upon valuing the pound sterling at $4.86, whereas in the last few months the value has fluctuated between $4.20 and $4.30, that is to say, the custom tax has been levied on $4.86 where the real cost of the article was only $4.25 on the average. Now, ! the suit made of that cloth costs more than $45, the customer is taxed again. So the cost of living is increased on the necessaries of life. The consumer is dissatisfied. The retailer is dissatisfied.

The taxes are complicated and the collection will be troublesome and expensive. They are taxes on business and production, and their tendency will be to lessen business and production. The retail merchant is forced into the position of a tax-collector, and instead of being paid for his labor, he will be put to additional expense, besides losing business.

fortune should be at the service of the State. Still more is it true that the State should have the right to take at least a share of fortunes accumulated by men out of the very necessities of war, by men who were safe and comfortable at home while young Canadians were suffering and dying in the trenches. The Government lets these accumulators of fortunes go free, while it taxes the veteran on his clothing and his boots. The Montreal Gazette, a Conservative Journal, says that the Minister of Finance has drawn the line too low, in the light of current prices, if his object is to exempt the clerical class and persons of modest means, in respect of clothing, and he discriminates in favor of the wealthy by taxing pianos 10 per cent., while the musical instrument of the poor, the gramaphone, is made to bear 20 per cent. It adds: Signs begin to point to the approach of a reaction, but a year or more may elapse before the suit which decently clothes a man drops to a figure near $45, or a durable pair of boots can be bought for $9. The basis of taxation taken by the Finance Minister is virtually a compulsory levy, unless one dresses in shoddy, and wears paper shoes, because it is not extravagance that prompts, but necessity that compels, the purchase of these articles above the taxed line. If prices greatly recede, the Minister can amend the legislation to meet the new condition, but in present circumstances his taxation falls equally upon the heavy and the light purse."

No mere patchwork will meet the public demand. The tariff needs to be revised and simplified, and this can be done only by a Government representing the people of Canada and the public opinion of the present time.

The Pose of Martyrdom

When it is said that the new taxes are unpopular, an attempt is made to place the Ministers in the position of martyrs to public duty. But who is asking them to sacrifice themselves at the shrine of duty? Who is forcing or urging them to remain in power? They are clinging to office in spite of every indication that the people are tired of them and longing for a change. The Unionist Government was formed for war purposes. Its man.

date from the electors, if it ever had any, has long since expired. Some of its most important members have resigned. Its majority has dwindled down from 70, as announced after the last general election, to the thirties, to the twenties, even as low as five. By the amendment moved to the Address at the opening of the session, it was invited to hold a general election, but it induced its followers to vote the motion down. And what was the inducement? With a considerable number of members it was simply the knowledge that they could not be re-elected, and therefore desired to postpone the general election as long as possible.

In the bye-elections the Government has received plain notice to quit. In Assiniboia, where the Government had a majority of 4,524 in 1917, it had no candidate in 1919. In Glengarry and Stormont, the Government candidate was elected by acclamation in 1917. In 1919 a United Farmer was elected by a large majority. In 1917 in North Ontario, the Government candidate was elected by more than 1,500. In 1919, a United Farmer was elected by a substantial majority. In Victoria and Carleton, N.B., the Hon. F. B. Carvell was elected as a Unionist by acclamation. In 1919 a Farmer was elected by about 3,500 majority.

In the last three bye-elections the Government continued to slide downhill. It had no candidate in Kamouraska and a Liberal was elected by acclamation. It had no candidate in the St. James Division of Montreal. The Liberal and Labor candidates there were equally hostile to the Government. The result in these two elections was Liberals two, Government none. In Temiskaming it had no regular candidate, and the Independent Conservative was at the bottom of the poll. He received a little more than 8,000 votes, while the Labor and Liberal candidates received nearly 8,600.

In the face of these plain demands to go, the Government announces that it will remain in office until 1922 or 1923. The friends of the Government may call this courage, the Toronto Globe calls it impudence, and the Globe was one of the strongest supporters of Union Government in 1917. The pose of martyrdom will excite only derision. "We are determined to remain in office for two or three years more in order that our sufferings may be prolonged: We enjoy unpopularity, and crave more of it." The public will

5

hardly believe it. A great campaign fund is being raised by the
profiteers. It is hoped that something may turn up between now
and 1922 or 1923 which may save the Government from accepting
the crown of martyrdom in the shape of a defeat in the next general elections. But unless the people are easily fooled, the hope
is vain.

The Profiteering Campaign Fund

The people of Canada have received fair warning of what is
in store for them in the next general election. The net is set in
sight of the bird. Mr. Ballantyne declares that the Government
will retain office until the last possible moment, and will then appeal to the country on the issue of moderate protection against free
trade. This will not be the reel issue. The real issue will be
between the profiteers and the people of Canada. It is announced that a huge campaign fund is to be raised by the beneficiaries
of the tariff. This fund, you may be sure, will not
be for the purpose of maintaining a tariff in which the public interest will be protected. It will be a profiteering fund. Where
will the money come from? From profits taken out of the pock-
ets of the people. What will the money be used for? To make
future profiteering secure. To frame a tariff in the interest of
the profiteers and at their dictation.

By announcing its determination to hang on to office until
1922 or 1923, the Government makes itself a party to the raising
and spending of the profiteering fund. If it intended to ask for a
verdict upon its own merits, it would go to the country at once.
There is no object in the delay, except to give time for the raising of the big fund and the propaganda which is to be financed by
the fund. The country is against the Government. It is to be

bought back, if the profiteers can do it. Free spontaneous opinion, as expressed in the movement of the Farmers and i[?] other ways, is to be fought by the lavish use of money. What is to be the answer of the non-profiteering classes of Canada to the challenge so impudently thrown down? Surely the only answer of men and women who think and have the courage of their convictions is to combine and fight the profiteers and the money power to which they so insolently appeal. With all their money, they can hope to win only by dividing the Liberals, the Farmers and the Labor men, who together compose an overwhelmingly majority of the people of Canada. The trick has been successfully played before, but never before was warning so plainly given. Never before was it said, "We intend to fool you. We need two years time to play out the game. We have several millions to spere out of the money we have taken out of you by profiteering, and we shall spend it in fooling or scaring you out of your honest convictions. The war which has slain or mained your sons has made us rich, and we shall use a little of our riches to protect the rest, and to make sure that the process of moneygetting is not disturbed in the future."

The big profiteering fund makes the issue clear, and indicates the nature of the campaign which ought to be fought by the friends of the people. Fight the Fund, should be the watchword. Meet the money power with the power of public opinion. Isolate the profiteers and keep them in the public eye as enemies of the people. Let there be no division among the the advocates of reform. Minor differences of opinion as to tariff reform should give way to the great issue. Shall the tariff be framed at the dictation of profiteers and in their interest or shall it be reformed by a reformed government representing a reformed Parliament, and expressing the free will and judgment of the electors of Canada?

The Government Petering Out

The result of the General Election of 1917, according to the Parliamentary Guide of 1918 (page 239) was a Government majority of 71, nearly two to one.

The Government majority on Mr. King's amendment, calling for a general election, was 34—less than one half the majority of 1917.

The Government majority on the budget was 26 in a House of 214—the figures being 120 to 94. Instead of being nearly two to one, as in 1917, it was little more than five to four.

More than once during the session the majority fell even lower than this—in one case to five. The majority is dwindling away. The Government is petering out. There would be a majority against the Government if it were not that many of its supporters know that they cannot be re-elected, and therefore wish to hang on as long as possible.

The bye-elections have gone steadily and heavily against the Government. It has lost Assiniboia, North Ontario, Victoria and Carleton, N.B., and Temiskaming, and gained nothing. It is afraid to hold an election in East Elgin. It has lost a large part of its support in the press. The Toronto Globe, which supported it so strongly in 1917, is now dead against it, nd declares that its announcement that it will remain in office until 1922 or 1923 is impudent. We quote:—

"It is an announcement impudent to the people of Canada. It it made on behalf of a Government which knows full well that in a general election there would not be enough of it left to sweep up. It voices the arrogance of a ministry that is afraid to bring on even a byeelection and of a Cabinet that accordingly is cluttered with "acting" heads of departments. It speaks for an Administration that is thoroughly aware that it has hopelessly forfeited the confidence of the country; that selfishly clings to office and endeavors to do things for which it has no public mandate."

Unrest and discontent in the country is increased by the conduct of the Government, at once timid and obstinate, in clinging to office after its mandate has expired.

Either Ignorant or Insolent

Fresh evidence of the Government's autocratic contempt for Parliament is found in the treatment of Mr. Sinclair's charge that $121,000,000 sent overseas had not been accounted for. The statement was not founded upon rumor. It was found in black and white in the Auditor General's report. The late Auditor General, Mr. Fraser, asked for vouchers as early as 1917, but obtained neither the vouchers nor any explanation regarding their absence. Mr. Sinclair said regarding this extraordinary state of affairs: "What has become of this $121,000,000? The Minister does not know; the Deputy does not know; the Auditor General does not know. There is apparently not a scrap of paper in the possession of the Government to show what has become of that $121,000,000." This was strictly true. If the Minister or any member of the Government knew, he did not think it worth while to give any explanation to the House of Commons. Mr. Sinclair did his duty in laying the facts before the House of Commons and giving the Government an opportunity to explain. The Government remained silent. Either it was ignorant of the facts, or it wilfully withheld them from Parliament.

Later on, the extraordinary situation was referred to by Mr. Archambault and by Dr. Michael Clark. Dr. Clark said "I hope whoever replies to me will give me come information as to where this mney is gone." The man who replied to Dr. Clark was Mr. Meighen, a minister who is regarded as a candidate for the leadership. He could give no information, though he "presumed" that the items were British or foreign credits, the accounting for which had not yet reached the Auditor General, and he said that if there was anything requiring explanation, the Public Accounts Committee was the place to inquire, and this Committee had not been called.

At last, on the first of June, eleven days after Mr. Sinclair spoke, Mr. Rowell came out with the explanation that the vouchers were in England, that they had not been sent to Canada because of the danger from German submarines, and that the auditing was being done in England. At once the question arises—why was not this explanation given immediately after Mr. Sinclair's speech? Was the Government itself ignorant of what had become of this huge sum of money, or did it consider that the House of Commons had no right to the information as to the expenditure of the people's money? Or did it wilfully withhold the information in order to enable Mr. Rowell to score a point in the closing hours of the debate? It looks like a case either of ignorance or insolence. The Government either did not know of any explanation until Mr. Rowell spoke, or it took the stand that it could hold the information until it suited its own purpose to give it, and that Parliament had no rights in the matter.

Mr. Rowell's lecture to the Opposition was beside the mark. Mr. Sinclair and the others who brought up the matter were performing a public duty. They made no false statement. They spoke, not upon rumors, but upon the official testimony of the Auditor-General, published for the information of Parliament. If that report conveyed a wrong impression, it was the duty of the Government at once to remove the impression. The explanation given by Mr. Rowell should have been given months ago, years ago; should at least have been given the moment Mr. Sinclair took his seat after making a statement of the highest importance. If the Government did not know what had become of this huge sum of money, it was ignorant and incompetent. If it did know, it was guilty of arrogant and insolent defiance of the rights of Parliament and the people.

Constitutional Reform

A newspaper report says that one name to be submitted to the caucus of Government supporters will be "the Constitutional Reform Party." Members who discussed it were practically unanimous in their opinion that such a name would meet the almost unanimous consent of the caucus.

"We have as much right to adopt this name as Sir John Macdonald had to adopt the name 'Confederation' in 1867," said one prominent Government supporter who was present at the discussion.

Other names suggested were "National party," "National Liberal-Conservative party," and "United Canadian party." It was fully agreed, according to the authority, that the term "union" shall be dropped entirely.

A party may call itself by any name it pleases. But why the party supporting the present Government should call itself a Constitutional Reform party, is a question hard to answer. The greatest constitutional reform effected in Canada was the establishment of responsible government carried by the Reformers, the predecessors of the Liberals. The Tories of that day fought teeth and nail against that reform, and described the Reformers as traitors who were really working for the separation of Canada from Great Britain. As was said at a Liberal gathering some time ago:

"On the other side Baldwin and Lafontaine succeeded because they had the right idea and stuck to it. They were called rebels and advocates of sedition. They refused to be frightened away from their guns by these cries and on the other hand they refused to be angered or provoked into any utterance which might give color to a charge of sedition or rebellion.

"The victory won by Baldwin and Lafontaine was good not only for Canada, but for the Empire. It allowed us to govern ourselves. It put an end to all friction between Canada and the British Government. It relieved British Ministers of all anxiety as to Canada. It laid the foundation of that system of self Government which now prevails all over the most contented and prosperous part of the British Empire. In recent years, it was vindicated signally in the case of South Africa. After the South African war, there was much hesitation about granting self government in that part of the world. But self government was granted and the action of the South African people in the recent war showed that this action was wise."

The Liberals are also the authors of another constitutional reform, provincial autonomy. It is well known that Sir John Macdonald at the time when confederation was proposed, preferred a legislative union—one Parliament for all Canada, and no Provincial Legislatures or Government. Look at the question from a practical as well as a constitutional point of view. Look at the immense volume of public business now transacted at Ottawa, the army of civil servants, the commissions, the sessions lengthening out to half or two-thirds of the year. Then ask yourself what would be the condition of affairs if all the public business now transacted at Toronto and Quebec, at Halifax and Edmonton, were piled up at Ottawa. The result would be congestion and chaos. The legislative and administrative machinery would be clogged, and some of the wheels might cease to turn. Instead of establishing an education bureau at Ottawa, we should be devising means of getting rid of some parts of the business already done here, and transferring it to the Provinces.

Neither in the past nor in the present has the Conservative

party any right to the name of Constitutional reform party. To-day, the Union Government is violating the spirit of the constitution, and standing for reaction instead of reform. Read what the President of the G. W. V. A. says:

"Parliament has denied to the electorate of Canada any opportunity since 1911 to assert their views upon domestic questions by means of the ballot.

"Parliament continues to ignore the fact that the demand for a general election does not arise solely from among returned soldiers, but is supported by the vast majority of those who have the interests of the country at heart, and who view with alarm the increasing unrest.

"Parliament has outlived its mandate."

The President says "Parliament," which is correct so far as the majority of the Members of the House is concerned, but Liberals have demanded an immediate general election, and voted for a resolution voicing that demand. There has been no election since 1911, under conditions allowing for the free expression of opinion on Canadian affairs. A soldier voting in France or England had no opportunity of studying Canadian affairs. Many of the returned soldiers, not having been 21 years of age in 1911, have never voted under fair conditions at all. No man under thirty has had such a chance to record his vote.

And this party, which now declares that there will be no election until 1922 or 1923, talks about inscribing on its banners the motto "Constitutional Reform," and its followers would describe themselves as Reformers, the good old name under which responsible government was won. Today the true Reformers and upholders of the constitution are the Liberals, who demand a return to responsible and representative government.

The Little Fellow's Chance

In one of the elections for President of the United States—probably in 1912—the writer visited a village in the State of New York, and he heard an American say that he was going to vote for Roosevelt because Roosevelt would give the little fellows a chance. The phrase somehow stuck in his memory, and today he can think of no better watchword for a party or a group or a combination of groups. The Little Fellow has long been waiting and fighting for his chance, and has too often been fooled out of it. The Big Interests have usually had their way, even in democratic countries like Canada, Great Britain and the United States. The Little Fellows have been divided by party feeling, by race antagonism, by religious prejudice; and by their divisions they have played into the hands of the Big Interests. Depend upon it, the same game will be played at the next general election in Canada. If the anti-French cry is played out, if the anti-American cry is played out, if the sectarian cry is played out, some other cry will be devised. Perhaps an attempt will be made to rally the cities and towns and villages against the farmers. Perhaps the workers in factories will be asked to give up a part of their wages for a campaign fund to fight the farmers. The game is to have the Little Fellows fight each other, while the Big Interests stand ready to take the fruits of the victory.

Today it looks as if the common people of Canada, the workers in fields and factories and stores, were on the verge of a victory for themselves. The Big Interests are profoundly alarmed. They are about to raise a huge campaign fund for publicity and propaganda. The propaganda, if we may judge by experience, will not be an appeal to reason. It will be an appeal to fear and prejudice, an attempt to divide the common people in order that the rule of the few may not be disturbed. Mr. Meighen says that the Liberals and the Farmers in Parliament are getting together "in order to pave the way for the great betrayal when the day comes, if it ever comes, that the united members are greater than the members behind the present Government.' The great betrayal! Betrayal of what or whom? Is a union of the advanced Liberals and the Farmers and the Labor men likely to result in a betrayal of the people? It is in the last degree improbable. If it is likely to result in a defeat of the profiteers, so much the better.

By this it is not meant that injustice should be done to any man rich or poor. What is meant is that Big Interest rule shall cease, and give place to rule by the common people, be they farmers or clerks, teachers or laborers, employing manufacturers or workers in factories or keepers of retail stores. This Canada in the past has been ruled too much by its so-called leaders in finance and industry and commerce. Some of these may have been able and conscientious men. Even so, their rule represented plutocracy, not democracy, and was therefore a rule not fitted for free and self-respecting men. The common people have obeyed the laws made under these conditions, and today they are seeking to change the conditions by peaceful, constitutional means. If they succeed, by the ballot, in taking government into their own hands, the Big Interests must in their turn loyally submit to the new conditions. They will be well advised to place their trust in the fairness and good sense of the common people, instead of trying to fight the ;·····. with big campaign funds.

The tariff issue today is not between free trade and protection, or between farmers and manufacturers and urban workers. The issue is whether the tariff shall be framed at the dictation of a few great interests, or revised in accordance with the will of the people working in stores and offices, in fields and factories. Is there to be a real democracy or a sham democracy, camouflaging plutocracy? It is for the people of Canada to say. They have only to unite and stand firm in order to have any kind of tariff and any kind of government they please, by the peaceful and constitutional methods which the ballot denotes. If they gain the power which is within their reach, let them be sane and fair; let them be zealous for construction and production, but zealous also for social justice.

Free Trade and Great Britain

Mr. Meighen says that Great Britain is selling three billion dollars worth of goods a year, and buying seven billion dollars worth, while the United States is selling eight billions and buying only three billions. Thus the "balance of trade" is against Great Britain and favorable to the United States; and therefore protection has benefited the United States and free trade has injured Great Britain.

It seems strange that the Minister should have overlooked the obvious fact that Great Britain sells less than the United States because it has less to sell; and buys more because in regard to food and other natural products it is unable to supply its own needs. In area the United States is comparable not with the British Islands, but with the whole of Europe, and the same is true of its natural resources and products. Unless it is argued that protection would increase the area of Great Britain or enable it to produce corn, cotton, petroleum, wheat and meat on the same scale as the United States, there is not a great deal in Mr. Meighen's position. It is the natural wealth of the United States that gives it any advantage it may possess over the British Islands. And the wonder is that these little islands have attained a position in the world, in industry, in commerce and in finance, far out of proportion to their size and natural resources.

. But when you compare the United States, not with Great Britain, but with continental Europe, you have an example of the enormous benefit of free trade. Europe is divided into sections by protective tariffs and by frontiers guarded by military power. The United States comprise a huge free trade area, over which all American products of farm, factory, mine and forest are freely exchanged. Producing every necessity of life in lavish abundance, and buying and selling freely over an area nearly as large as Europe, how could the United States fail to prosper under any kind of tariff? On the other hand, Europe today is suffering from the effect of trade restriction, which aggravates the destructive consequences of war. The Supreme Council at the Peace Conference says:—"Governments must co-operate in the reconstruction of the commercial economic life of Europe, which is vitally interrelated by facilitating the regular interchange of their products and by avoiding arbitrary obstruction of the natural flow of European trade."

Great Britain overcomes its natural disadvantages by drawing freely upon the wealth of the world. Its position today is the proof of the wisdom of that policy.

The World Needs Economic Peace
The Manchester Guardian says:—

"What was urgently wanted in November, 1918, was to get to

work at once on the economic regeneration of Europe. Tonnage in millions had been sunk. The product of men's labor had been blown into the air to the value of thousands of millions of pounds. It could not but be that the world would be poorer, and its greater poverty would be expressed primarily and most markedly in a shortage of food and raw material extracted from the earth. Here the greatest dislocation of industry had taken place, for it was in particular the peasants drawn from the land who had made so large a part of the Continental armies. But if Europe had been at once restored to peace much might have been done even in the course of 1919, to get the economic machine into working order again."

The Guardian goes on to criticize European statesmen for delaying the restoration of peace, and among other things for encouraging war with Russia, "in the vain attempt to impose upon Russia a reactionary Government which she would not have." Canada, in spite of the recent talk about her new "voice" in foreign affairs has very little to say about the settlement of Europe. It is Europeans, after all, who must govern Europe. We in Canada can assist in the process of restoring Europe by maximum production and by the freest possible exchange of products.

In a word, we must now reverse the methods of war. For more than four years most of the European nations were engaged in destruction and conflict. The remedy for the evils so occasioned is intense concentration on construction and co-operation. Trade between nations is a form of co-operation and trade cannot be one-sided. There is a good deal of talk about Canada finding foreign markets, but importation from foreign countries is regarded by doctrinaire protectionists as an evil to be avoided. Obviously, if we keep on encouraging exports and discouraging imports, the effect must be to increase scarcity in Canada and make the high cost of living higher, as well as to deprive the country of its revenue on imports.

High tariff protection is really a continuation of the processes of war. During the war the nations engaged in the conflict were busily engaged in obstructing the trade of their enemies. Germany and Austria Hungary were blockaded, and the

German submarines tried to prevent food from reaching England.
When trade is obstructed by tariffs, the effect is the same as that
of blockades and submarines.

What is wanted today is a policy that will make food and
other necessaries of life more abundant. The right policy for
that purpose consists in greater production and freer exchange.
In Canada we need more people on the land. The Liberal tariff
policy aims at reducing the cost of living in two ways. The Fielding amendment says: —

"That in view of the continued increase in the high cost of
living, of the greatly increased burden of taxation, of the hardship which many of the people suffer from these causes, and the
unrest naturally arising therefrom; and in view of the desirability of adopting measures to increase production and effect
such relief to the consumers and producers as may be within the
power of Parliament, the House is of opinion that, pending a
wider revision of the tariff, substantial reductions of the burdens
of customs taxation should be made with a view to the accomplishing of two purposes of the highest importance; first, diminishing
the very high cost of living which presses so severely on the
masses of the people; second, reducing the cost of the instruments
of production in the industries based on the natural resources of
the Dominion, the vigorous development of which is essential to the
progress and prosperity of our country.

The talk about economic war after the war is sheer nonsense.
What the world needs today above all things is economic peace,
production instead of destruction, and co-operation instead of
conflict. There is not the slightest danger of Canada being flooded by cheap European products. Europe is suffering, not from
abundance, but from scarcity of the necessities of life and the
means of production. The sooner European industry is restored
the better for Canada.

Clothing Not a Luxury

Under the new budget, the excess profits tax is reduced, and
the taxation imposed upon the masses of the people is increased.
The latter process is camouflaged by describing necessaries of life

17

as luxuries, though it is true that some luxuries are taxed also. Common sense revolts at the notion of classing hats, boots and shoes, underwear, coats, waistcoats, and trousers as luxuries, merely because they are of fairly good quality. Sensible people have been in the habit of buying as good clothing as they could afford, not for purposes of luxury, and ostentation, but for comfort and wearing qualities.

The taxes, as Mr. McMaster points out, bear with peculiar severity on persons living on fixed salaries, the purchasing power of which has been greatly diminished by price inflation. Teachers, for instance, are notoriously underpaid, and have found it extremely difficult to keep up the decent appearance which their duties demand, and which is an important element in the maintenance of discipline and influence over children.

In effect, the new taxes amount to a reduction of their already small incomes. The purchasing power of those incomes is impaired. The high cost of living is made higher by the new taxes. Clerks in stores and offices are obliged to maintain a certain standard in dress. The new taxation docks a considerable amount off their salaries.

The policy of restriction of trade, which was formerly applied only to imports, now strikes at the domestic commerce of the country. The tax gatherer stands at the door of every retail merchant in Canada, from the great departmental store to the smallest establishment, and demands his toll. An enormously expensive and troublesome machinery will have to be devised for checking sales and preventing evasion. The ultimate consumer, of course, will have to pay in the long run, but the business of the merchant will be hampered, and his expenses increased.

The country will view with dismay a further increase in the ranks of officialdom. There is too much government, too much interference with individual liberty and initiative. While there is a general demand for more production, there is a constant increase in the ranks of the non-productive classes, and this tendency will be increased by the necessity for inspection, supervision and clerical work which the new taxation will create.

What is required is a tariff that will encourage commerce and industry, and free the energies of the people instead of hampering them. Taxation needs to be simplified, not further complicated. The Government shirks the duty of real tariff revision, and seeks to put the people off with makeshifts and irritating restrictions upon trade.

The Government's Narrow Escape

The division in the House of Commons on May 17, when the Government majority was reduced to five, was a remarkable event. The vote was taken on Mr. Fielding's resolution "That this house desires to record its opinion that, before any arrangement is made, the house should be fully informed concerning any negotiations between the Imperial or United States governments and the Government of Canada, and that the matter should be submitted to the House of Commons, and all correspondence connected therewith should be laid on the table of the house."

Mr. Fielding made it clear that he was not expressing any opinion as to the merits or demerits of the new departure, which would be discussed at a future time. He was protesting against the taking of action by the Government without consulting Parliament and without information being given to Parliament. There had been too much government by order-in-council. There was a tendency to magnify the powers of the Government and to minimise the powers of Parliament. The true view was that Government was only a committee of Parliament. There are times when encroachments on Parliamentary authority are excused upon the plea of a crisis or emergency demanding swift action. In this case there was no such crisis or emergency. There was no public interest that would suffer by delay. Practically there had been no public discussion of the question. No candidate had made an issue of the question of representation at Washington.

Mr. Rowell, in his reply, enlarged upon the importance of the trade relations between Canada and the United States; and Sir Robert Borden quoted a British Ambassador at Washington as saying that three-fourths of the business done by the British Embassy at Washington was Canadian business. All this may be admitted. There is undoubtedly need for a better system of transacting Canadian business at Washington. But the very importance of the question is a reason for giving Parliament that infor-

nation and opportunity for discussion which Mr. Fielding's resolution demands. Mr. Rowell quoted the Winnipeg Free Press
as supporting the position of the Government. In reply to this,
Mr. King quoted an article in the Free Press, published within
the last few days, in which the position taken was practically that
of Mr. Fielding and the Opposition.

The Free Press says that there can be no intelligent comment
until more information is available—that it will be the duty of
Parliament to submit the arrangement to very keen scrutiny. It
asks several questions about the nature of the arrangement.

"Our representative is to be known as a minister. Will he be
accepted as a minister by the State Department at Washington?
Will he be a member of the diplomatic corps, having all the rights,
powers, immunities and privileges enjoyed by the ministers of all
other countries represented at Washington? Will he be the equal
in diplomatic statute of, let us say, the minister from Venezuela?
Or will his position at Washington be actually undefined with a
mere courtesy status? Parliament and the country will need conclusive answer to these and similar questions; and not until this
information is supplied will it be possible to say whether this is
a step forward or backward. It is asserted in certain quarters that
this marks an enlarg ment of Canadian powers and that it is another step forward on the road to nationhood. The Government
at Ottawa no doubt believes that this will be the effect of the inno-
vation. But we regard with some trepidation formal arrange-
ments entered into three years after the adoption of a declared policy of equality of status between all the British nations by which
it is possible that Canada may accept, ratify, and confirm a status
of admitted diplomatic inferiority, formally putting her name to
documents that confirm this subordination. If the Canadian minister at Washington is only a camouflaged chief clerk or a com-
missioner, it would be better to have no minister there.

"If his position there is by courtesy, if Canada cannot endow
her representative with all the powers which other ministers enjoy,
then Canada should send no one to Washington until she can vest
him with the true prerogative of office.

"Information upon these extremely important points is lacking;
until it is forthcoming any conclusive judgment upon the wisdom

or otherwise of the Government's action is not possible. But the matter is of great importance and Parliament should regard it as one of its prime duties to see that the matter is fully discussed from all angles and in the light of full knowledge."

When Sir George Foster made his announcement as to the new departure, he said that all available papers would be brought down as quickly as possible. Mr. Archambault pointed out that a distinct promise of information was given by Mr. Rowell:— "There are certain confidential communications between the Prime Minister of Canada and the Imperial Government. Negotiations are not yet closed. As soon as they are closed I am sure the Prime Minister will lay the whole matter before the House, but he is conducting negotiations personally in Great Britain.

But Sir Robert Borden flatly refused to give the information. He said that he had examined the correspondence carefully, and that it could not be brought down without detriment to the public interest. This, said Mr. King, is a bad beginning in a new departure, if our foreign policy is to be bound up with secrecy from the start. "We're driving right into the very vortex that created the whole situation in Europe, going against the very thing which the Allied nations have been urging so strongly, namely—that diplomacy should not be secret. Why, Sir, if in a matter which concerns the relations between the different parts of the Empire, between different nations, we start off by informing the people's representatives in Parliament that they cannot be told one word in regard to the conditions which have brought about their all-important change, what may we expect as the result of such diplomacy?"

Mr. Fielding's resolution, as was said during the debate, brought concretely before the House the question of the supremacy of Parliament or the autocracy of the Government, and the Government narrowly escaped defeat. When the question comes up again, and the status of the new representative is discussed, some important questions must be answered. As the Winnipeg Free Press says, it would be better to have no minister at Washington than a camouflaged chief clerk. Canada should be worthily represented by a Canadian whose information and ability will make him an authority on Canadian affairs. But the wisdom of giving the Canadian minister power to manage affairs that are not Canadian when the British Ambassador is absent, is doubtful

What is the reason that the Government could muster only 68 votes against the Fielding resolution, escaping defeat by a majority of only five? Either many of its supporters were in favor of the resolution, or they have become dissatisfied or indifferent as to the fate of the Government. It is likely that the general unpopularity of the Government, as manifested in the country, has worked its way into the minds and hearts of its supporters in the House. A good many members, as is well known, have no hope of being re-elected, and have been voting on the Government side in order to delay the hour when they must abandon their seats in the House. But this is not a very inspiring motive, and may be weakened by weariness and dissatisfaction. We have a tired Government with a tired Parliamentary following. It would be an act of mercy to put both of them out of their misery.

No Patchwork Alliance Wanted

Sir John Simon, a leading member of the British Liberal party, dealt recently with a proposal for a Liberal-Tory combination against "rampant Socialism." He said that he found it quite impossible to believe in such a combination.

It was a policy, he believed, which was not likely to stop or hinder, but to promote and in some minds justify, a more extreme Socialist doctrine. It was, on the other hand, a course which, whatever else it promised, did not promise a very happy future for Liberals. He would make this simple proposition to Coalition Liberals—the future of Coalition Liberalism was Toryism.

"And what a moment was this to ask Liberals to abandon the traditions of their Liberal birthright. We were living in a world which was longing, more than anything else, for the reality and certainty of peace. The League of Nations was only a skeleton to be clothed with flesh and blood, but it was Liberalism, and only Liberalism, which could make the League of Nations a real and vital thing. Liberals were the only guardians of the policy of peace conceived as a high duty and a high ideal for mankind.

"There are thousands of people in this country," concluded the speaker, "who are looking to see whether there remains a creed, a faith, alive and active, which is able, with justice to all classes, to develop the future of our community. It can be done by the mediatory, reconciling, progressive spirit of pure Liberalism. It can be done by nothing else on earth, and I call upon you who believe in the potent force, the urgent need of the application of Liberal doctrine and practice, to join with me in vowing we will maintain ourselves as a separate combination of free men and women who have no axe to grind, no favor to solicit, and who believe that in argument and democracy the future of this country is secure."

A similar line was taken by Mr. Asquith. He said:—"My counsel to you is to keep faithful to your old traditions, to safeguard and vivify your organization and never lose sight of that saving quality which alone makes politics a reputable profession for honorable men, that a party exists not to keep power, not to acquire power, but it exists for the promotion of great and worthy ideals."

"Just think," Mr. Asquith continued, "in a situation such as this, what would have been the attitude of men like Mr. Gladstone? Do you think they would have allowed themselves to be scared by the bogey of Bolshevism into furling the old flag and marching, with bowed head and reversed arms, horse, foot and artillery, into the camp of the enemy?"

This is good advice. What Great Britain wants today is not another patch work combination between Liberals and Tories, but a revival of the Liberal party, with a policy that is neither 'rampant" nor reactionary. The talk of "Bolshevism" and 'rampant Socialism" is merely a device for keeping Liberals in the Tory camp. The best safeguard against Bolshevism is a strong, progressive Liberal party, open-minded, hospitable to new ideas, but proceeding along moderate, constitutional lines. The same remark applies to Canada. One of the devices for patching is a proposal for the formation of a "safe and sane" party to combat extreme ideas. The real object is to perpetuate Toryism, under a new name, and to scare a section of the Liberal party by representing that Bolshevism is making great headway in Canada. Farmers, labor men, free traders and advanced thinkers of all kinds are lumped together as Bolshevists. Some time ago, a motion picture was shown in Toronto for the purpose of depicting the horrors of Bolshevism. It bore all the marks of propaganda, and was supported in part by subscriptions from some wealthy men. The people refused to be horrified, and the performance fell flat.

The scare is not justifiable. Canada is poor ground for Bolshevism or any kind of revolutionary doctrine. There is a good deal of unrest and discontent, wh ' h is largely due to the existence at Ottawa of a government and Parliament that no longer represent the people. The Liberal party does not require to enter into any Tory alliance, in order to present a policy that is at once sane and progressive. The true rallying ground for moderate and progressive men is the Liberal party itself. If it maintains its organization and is true to its traditions, it will attract to itself men of that stamp from all the other parties and groups.

No such basis can be found either in Unionism or in such a revival of old fashioned Toryism as Mr. Rogers proposes. Unionism is regarded by the country at large as an extinct force, and its name would be a source of weakness. Toryism would be regarded as reactionary, and would repel progressive and advanced thinkers, and tend to drive them into the ranks of extremists. What is wanted to restore confidence in the institutions of the country is not a combination of privilege and prejudice backed up by a ruge campaign fund, but a return to responsible and representative government, the election of a House of Commons that will eally represent the country, and the formation of a Government of he same kind.

A General Recall Wanted

In a recent debate in the House of Commons, the opinion most generally expressed was that the recall was undemocratic and against the spirit of our constitution, because it interfered with the free exercise of the private judgment of a member of Parliament, and made him a mere delegate or agent of a few men in one constituency, instead of a representative of the whole nation.

There may be some force in this, but many of our exesting practices are equally adverse to the independent exercise of the independent judgment of a member of Parliament. They escape

24

notice because we are accustomed to them, while the recall attracts attention by its novelty. It is not always realised that every member of Parliament is now subject to recall by the Government of the day. The regular duration of Parliament is five years; but at any period before the expiration of that term the Government may advise a dissolution, and force the members of the House of Commons to go back for re-election if they desire to continue to represent their constituencies.

Or, if it suits the convenience of the Government, it may cling to office and prolong the life of Parliament when there is every indication that the people want a change. Such is the present position. The Government was returned to power as a Union Government to carry out war measures. The war is at an end. Whatever reason there may have been for the coalition in 1917, that reason has now ceased to exist. The bye-elections have gone overwhelmingly against the Government. Some of its most influential supporters in the press have condemned it. It is almost without representation in the Maritime Provinces and in Quebec. What the country needs today is not the individual recall, applying to a single member here and there, but a general recall of the whole House of Commons, giving the people an opportunity to elect a body that will represent it upon the issues of the day.

Canadian Minister at Washington

It is at last stated with authority that Canada is to have a representative at Washington. Sir George Foster has announced in the House that an agreement has been reached between the Canadian and British Governments. A minister plenipotentiary will have charge of Canadian affairs and will at all times be the ordinary channel of communication with the United States Government in matters of purely Canadian concern, acting upon instructions from and reporting direct to the Canadian Government. In the absence of the Ambassador the Canadian minister will take charge of the whole Embassy and of the representation of Imperial as well as Canadian interests.   He will be accredited by His Majesty to the President with the necessary powers for the purpose.   Sir George Foster adds:—

"The need for this important step has been fully realised by both Governments for some time.   For a good many years there has been direct communication between Washington and Ottawa, but the constantly increasing importance of Canadian interests in the United States has made it apparent that Canada should be represented there in some distinctive manner, for this would doubtless tend to expedite negotiations, and naturally first-hand acquaintance with Canadian conditions would promote good understanding.   In view of the peculiarly close relations that have always existed between the people of Canada and those of the United States, it is confidently expected as well that this new step will have the very desirable result of maintaining and strengthening the friendly relations and co-operation between the British Empire and the United States."

There can be no doubt of the importance of Canadian relations with the United States, and of the need for more direct communication.   The leader of the Opposition, however, pointed out that Parliament ought to have been made aware of the negotiations before they were concluded.   The case affords another instance of the manner in which the Government ignores Parliament and encroaches upon its authority.

In 1911, Sir George Foster, in discussing the free wheat provisions of the proposed reciprocity agreement between Canada and the United States, said: "If this sort of thing goes into operation under the glare and glitter and glamor of a promised fabulous rise of prices for the products of which the U. S. exports its surplus, there will be disappointment keen and bitter.   I hope our farmers will never be subjected to the risk of that disappointment."

In his peroration, he said, referring to the whole agreement, "this proposal cuts our country into sections, and at every section bleeds the life blood from it," And again, "Like Samson, we would arise and would shake ourselves and find that our strength is gone.   I utter the most solemn words I have ever uttered in my life, and I believe them to the very bottom of my heart, that there is danger and deep danger ahead.''

However, it is better to rejoice over Sir George Foster's conversion to sounder views than to reproach him for what he said in 1911. He has been mellowed by age. His Government, during the war and the succeeding months, has had very close relations with the United States. If we are to have a Minister at Washington, and if his mission is to be beneficial, the spirit governing our relations must be very different from that which actuated the bitter opposition to the reciprocity agreement of 1911.

The Rogers Movement

While Sir Robert Borden's return to Ottawa is associated with the vision of a permanent Unionist party, the Rogers movement for the revival of old-time Toryism makes headway. A meeting has been held at Toronto, with a view to making preparations for a convention of Liberal Conservatives at Ottawa, ''for the purpose of selecting a leader,'' and dealing with other matters. Evidently the leadership of Sir Robert Borden is not recognized. One of the resolutions adopted at the meeting was in these words:—

''That, in the opinion of this conference of Dominion-wide Liberal-Conservatives, the time has arrived to perfect organisation in all the provinces of Canada, and through such organisation prepare to enable those who believe in the traditional policy of Sir John Macdonald and Sir George Etienne Cartier to register their opinion at the impending general election of that great policy that has stood the test in the fire of common-sense for forty years and made Canada what it is today—a policy that during that long period has ever been the pathfinder to progress and to harmony between all the provinces, along ways where liberty and good-feeling foster and preserve our Canadian heritage for our own Canadian people as an integral part of the British Empire.''

What is meant by the traditional policy of Macdonald and Cartier? These statesmen dealt with the problems of their own day, doing some good and making some mistakes, as most public men do. It is well to study the history of Canada and read the biographies of its statesmen for instruction, example and warning, but it must be remembered that the Canada of the early days of Confederation was a very different country from the Canada of today. At that time we were vainly calling for immigrants to come in and settle our lands. Later on the immigrants came in large numbers, and now there is talk of the danger of admitting them too freely, of the necessity of educating them as Canadian citizens, and of withholding the franchise from those of certain races. The war has created problems such as were not dreamed of even by men of the broadest vision a generation ago. The growth of Canadian industries and industrial centres has brought us face to face with the labor problem.

Macdonald and Cartier are credited with the desire for harmony, among the provinces, liberty and good feeling. Since the death of Sir John Macdonald the party which he led has strayed away from this path, and the result is that Quebec is practically unrepresented in the Government, and on the Government side of the House. Mr. Rogers, perhaps, is calling for a return to the policy of Macdonald and Laurier; but his party contains elements that are antagonistic to harmony. As to preserving our Canadian heritage for the Canadian people, we are all in favor of that. It is at least a theory on which all agree, though in practice a good deal of the "heritage" has fallen into the hands of a favored few. Another resolution expresses dissatisfaction with the present state of affairs at Ottawa:—

"That, if Canada is to grow and prosper, the present ambiguity and vacillation in the national council of our country must give place to the definite and firm practices which will alone make for stability of government and assure us the adequate development of our great mineral wealth and render available for manufacture Canada's natural resources, thereby placing our producers in a position equal to their competitors in all parts of the world, and likewise to achieve the mastery of our domestic markets, with a surplus for the expansion of our export trade. We have within our boundaries every natural product necessary for industrial development, and every commodity for the needs of a great nation. This is the time to grasp our opportunities with decision and with determination. The time for the Liberal-Conservative party to work out through safe and sound methods how best the present policy of continuous borrowing with scarcely any provision made for the repayment of enormous obligations may be replaced by an economic program through which, with the aid of our tremendous natural resources, we may look forward to carrying lightly our heavy war indebtedness and, at the same time, feel that in the future we shall have pride and satisfaction that our currency, our finance, our industry, our agriculture and our people will stand pre-eminent."

According to this Conservative testimony there is ambiguity and vacillation in the national councils, and there is continuous borrowing with scarcely any provision made for the repayment of enormous obligations. And what is the remedy? The people of Canada are asked by one faction to wait for the resurrection of the old Conservative party, and by another faction to wait for the patching up of the ramshackle structure of the Unionist party. Surely the party which is in this disorganized condition ought to be content to accept a term in opposition, there to do its reorganising and patching, and not to pretend to lead and govern the country until it has arranged the affairs of its own household. To ask the country to wait until the Conservative or Unionist party makes up its mind as to its own character and policy is a proposal so cool that it may almost be called impudent. The constitutional remedy for the muddle is a change of Government, made in accordance with a general election which will represent public opinion as it is today. The time has passed for any sort of reconstruction to be accomplished by men now holding office or their supporters. The work of reconstruction must be done by the electors of Canada and the representatives whom they freely choose. The country needs such a change as was made in 1896 when "vacillation and ambiguity" gave place to vigor and steadiness.

The Franchise and Citizenship

Some votes in the House on the Franchise Bill illustrated the age-long conflict between Liberalism and Toryism. The Liberals were in favor of a broader franchise, the Tories were in favor of a narrower franchise. The situation in Canada in 1920 is like the situation in England nearly a hundred years ago. A century ago the franchise in England was regarded not as a right, but as a privilege. Great manufacturing cities were deprived of the franchise, because the mechanics who created the prosperity of these cities were not regarded as the equals of the voters who bowed and scraped before the aristocrats who owned the right to represent the "rotten boroughs." The issue today and was nearly a hundred years ago, is "Shall the people rule?"

It is to be regretted that it fell to the lot of Mr. Guthrie to proclaim the Tory doctrine that the franchise is a conferred right—that the government of the day shall have the right to say, in an arbitrary way, who shall vote and who shall not vote. Mr. Guthrie, it has been said, has good Liberal blood in his veins, and has not parted company with all his Liberal ideas. But the notion that the franchise is a privilege graciously conceded by the "upper classes" to the "lower classes" is a Tory and reactionary idea. It is true that Parliament, as the law-making body, must regulate the franchise, must say who is to vote and who is not to vote. That must be decided by somebody. But the duty cast upon Parliament is not that of a lord and master, granting or refusing privileges to its obedient servants, the people. Its duty is that of a servant of the people, or at least of that of an umpire or a referee endeavoring to decide according to the best of his judgment, who should compose the electorate.

A century ago the right to vote, or rather the power to vote, was restricted to a very small number of persons in the United Kingdom. We need not refer to Canada, which was then in its infancy. The Reform Bill of the early thirties of the nineteenth century enlarged the list of voters. This was not a favor, graciously granted to the people by Parliament. It was a confession that those who had previously regulated the franchise were wrong, that a wrong had been done to men who had the right to vote, but who had been deprived by unjust laws of the power to vote.

After the Reform Bill, the franchise was enlarged from time to time both in Great Britain and in Canada, until at last the basis became practically manhood suffrage. But the notion that the Crown, or Government, or Parliament, was doling out these enlargements as a sort of bounty or charity to the people, is as wrong as wrong can be. What really happened was that the servants of the people were gradually becoming educated by the growth of democratic ideas. They once had the idea that the few should rule. They were with difficulty convinced that a somewhat larger number should rule, or should have some say in the manner in which they should be governed. They are not yet aware of the fact that they are only servants of the people and that the phrase "sovereign people" is one of real significance. The so-called governing classes are to some extent under the influence of the idea which in recent years we have been condemning as Prussian—the idea of State-worship. In this kind of worship they regard themselves as high-priests of the temple.

Until very recent years women were excluded from the franchise. When Parliament gives them the franchise, it does not bestow a favor, nor does it merely acknowledge that women have prepared themselves for the franchise and are now capable of exercising it, of doing what they were not qualified to do ten years ago. What the Parliament of today does, is to confess that its predecessors were wrong. It is not that women have improved and become educated and qualified for the exercise of the franchise. It is that Parliament itself has become educated, and has perceived and confessed that the exclusion of women from the franchise was wrong.

The great principle underlying the present franchise law is that all men and women shall vote—that the basis of the franchise shall be humanity. Still there are members and members of Parliament who cling to the notion that they are dispensing a sort of charity when they allow men and women to vote—that they are political almsgivers—that they have the right to pick and choose and say who is to vote and who is not to vote. The pretension is all the more ridiculous when it is remembered that the present Government and the members of Parliament upon whose support it relies are mere usurpers, who in a fair and democratic election would be shorn of their power by the voice of the people.

The franchise law contains a lot of pedantic rubbish about "aliens," which the Liberals and other progressive members of the House have tried to clear away. The House of Commons, not as a despotic ruler, but as a trustee for the people, may have a right to associate good citizenship with the franchise. Good citizenship is not a matter of race or birth. It is a matter of conduct. It is a

9 780260 021472